The Economic Impact of S. 744, the Border Security, Economic Opportunity, and Immigration Modernization Act

Summary

The Border Security, Economic Opportunity, and Immigration Modernization Act (S. 744) would revise laws governing immigration and the enforcement of those laws, allowing for a significant increase in the number of noncitizens who could lawfully enter the United States permanently or temporarily.[1] The bill also would create a process for many currently unauthorized residents to gain legal status, subject to their meeting conditions specified in the bill. The Congressional Budget Office (CBO) and the staff of the Joint Committee on Taxation (JCT) have prepared an estimate of the cost of that legislation to the federal government, including projections of the bill's effects on both federal spending and federal revenues.[2]

That cost estimate reflects some, but not all, of the effects that S. 744 would have on the economy. This supplemental report provides estimates of the overall economic impact of the legislation and of the incremental federal budgetary effects of changes in the economy that the cost estimate does not reflect. Ascertaining the effects of immigration policies on the economy and the federal budget is complicated and highly uncertain, even in the short run, and that task is even more difficult for longer periods; for that reason, this report addresses the next 20 years but does not attempt to look over a longer horizon.

---

1. This analysis addresses the version of the bill that was reported by the Senate Committee on the Judiciary on May 28, 2013, including the amendments made in the star print of June 6, 2013.

2. See Congressional Budget Office, cost estimate for S. 744, the Border Security, Economic Opportunity, and Immigration Modernization Act (June 18, 2013), www.cbo.gov/publication/ 44225. That estimate includes an analysis of the mandates that the bill would impose on state, local, and tribal governments (as mandates are defined in the Unfunded Mandates Reform Act), but like CBO's other cost estimates, it does not assess all of the effects that the bill would have on the budgets of such governments.

How Would the Economic Impact of the Legislation Affect Federal Budget Deficits?

Cost estimates produced by CBO and JCT typically reflect the convention that macroeconomic variables such as gross domestic product (GDP) and employment remain fixed at the values they are projected to reach under current law. That is a long-standing convention—one that has been followed in the Congressional budget process since it was established in 1974. However, because S. 744 would significantly increase the size of the U.S. labor force, assuming that total employment was unchanged would imply that any employment of the additional immigrants would be offset one-for-one by lower employment elsewhere in the population. Because that outcome would be highly implausible, CBO and JCT relaxed the assumption of fixed GDP and employment and incorporated into the cost estimate their projections of the legislation's direct effects on the U.S. population, employment, and taxable compensation. Nevertheless, to remain as consistent as possible with the estimating rules CBO and JCT follow for almost all other legislation, the cost estimate for S. 744 does not incorporate the budgetary impact of every economic consequence of the bill.

The analysis here provides an estimate of the incremental budgetary effects that would arise from the economic outcomes that are not reflected in the cost estimate. Specifically, it includes some additional budgetary effects stemming from changes in the productivity of labor and capital, the income earned by capital, the rate of return on capital (and therefore the interest rates on government debt), and the differences in wages for workers with different skills. CBO estimates that an increase in productivity and capital income would reduce the bill's federal budgetary cost but that an increase in the interest rates on government debt—and thus an increase in interest payments—would raise the budgetary cost, as would changes in the relative wages of people at various points in the skill distribution, although only modestly.

On balance, the economic impacts not included in the cost estimate would have no significant net effect on federal budget deficits during the coming decade and would reduce deficits during the following decade. Taking into account a limited set of economic effects, the cost estimate shows that changes in direct spending and revenues under the legislation would *decrease* federal budget deficits by $197 billion over the 2014–2023 period and by roughly $700 billion over the 2024–2033 period. The cost estimate also shows that implementing the legislation would result in net discretionary costs of $22 billion over the 2014–2023 period and $20 billion to $25 billion over the 2024–2033 period, assuming appropriation of the amounts authorized or otherwise needed to implement the legislation.[3] According to CBO's central estimates (within a range that reflects the uncertainty about two key economic relationships in CBO's analysis), the economic impacts *not* included in the cost estimate would have no further net effect on budget deficits over the 2014–2023

---

3. Those additional appropriations would depend on future actions by lawmakers, and because the total amount of discretionary funding is currently capped through 2021 by the Budget Control Act of 2011, extra funding for the purposes of this legislation might lead to lower funding for other purposes rather than larger deficits.

period and would further reduce deficits (relative to the effects reported in the cost estimate) by about $300 billion over the 2024–2033 period.[4]

How Would the Legislation Affect the Economy?

S. 744 would boost economic output. Taking account of all economic effects (including those reflected in the cost estimate), the bill would increase real (inflation-adjusted) GDP relative to the amount CBO projects under current law by 3.3 percent in 2023 and by 5.4 percent in 2033, according to CBO's central estimates.[5] Compared with GDP, gross national product (GNP) per capita accounts for the effect on incomes of international capital flows and adjusts for the number of people in the country.[6] Relative to what would occur under current law, S. 744 would lower per capita GNP by 0.7 percent in 2023 and raise it by 0.2 percent in 2033, according to CBO's central estimates. Per capita GNP would be less than 1 percent lower than under current law through 2031 because the increase in the population would be greater, proportionately, than the increase in output; after 2031, however, the opposite would be true.

CBO's central estimates also show that average wages for the entire labor force would be 0.1 percent *lower* in 2023 and 0.5 percent *higher* in 2033 under the legislation than under current law. Average wages would be slightly lower than under current law through 2024, primarily because the amount of capital available to workers would not increase as rapidly as the number of workers and because the new workers would be less skilled and have lower wages, on average, than the labor force under current law. However, the rate of return on capital would be higher under the legislation than under current law throughout the next two decades.

The estimated reductions in average wages and per capita GNP for much of the next two decades do not necessarily imply that current U.S. residents would be worse off, on average, under the legislation than they would be under current law. Both of those figures represent differences between the averages for *all* U.S. residents under the legislation—including both the people who would be residents under current law and the additional people who would come to the country under the legislation—and the

---

4. The total estimated cost of S. 744 to the federal budget is represented by the sum of the costs reported in the cost estimate and the effects on deficits arising from the economic impacts *not* included in the cost estimate that are reported here. Following long-standing conventions of the Congressional budget process, CBO reports those figures separately.

5. For CBO's baseline (current-law) economic projections, see Congressional Budget Office, *The Budget and Economic Outlook: Fiscal Years 2013 to 2023* (February 2013), www.cbo.gov/publication/43907. Those projections extend to 2023. For the purposes of drawing comparisons in this analysis, CBO extended its economic projections beyond 2023 by projecting GDP to grow at the same rate as it did in the economic benchmark in CBO's latest long-term projections. See Congressional Budget Office, *The 2012 Long-Term Budget Outlook* (June 2012), www.cbo.gov/publication/43288. Economic estimates in this report are given on a calendar-year basis.

6. Unlike the more commonly cited GDP, GNP primarily excludes foreigners' earnings on investments in the U.S. economy but includes U.S. residents' earnings overseas; changes in GNP are therefore a better measure of the effects of policies on U.S. residents' income than are changes in GDP.

averages under current law for people who would be residents in the absence of the legislation. As noted, the additional people who would become residents under the legislation would earn lower wages, on average, than other residents, which would pull down the average wage and per capita GNP; at the same time, the income earned by capital would increase. CBO has not analyzed the full economic effects of the legislation separately for the incomes of people who would be U.S. residents under current law.

In sum, relative to current law, enacting S. 744 would:

- Increase the size of the labor force and employment,
- Increase average wages in 2025 and later years (but decrease them before that),
- Slightly raise the unemployment rate through 2020,
- Boost the amount of capital investment,
- Raise the productivity of labor and of capital, and
- Result in higher interest rates.

Employment and Wages. The supply of labor in the economy would increase primarily because the legislation would loosen or eliminate annual limits on various categories of permanent and temporary immigration.[7] Enacting the bill would, in CBO's view, increase the U.S. population by about 10 million people (about 3 percent) in 2023 and by about 16 million people (about 4 percent) in 2033.

CBO and JCT expect that new immigrants of working age would participate in the labor force at a higher rate, on average, than other people in that age range in the United States. Relative to CBO's projections under current law, enacting the bill would increase the size of the labor force by about 6 million (about 3½ percent) in 2023 and by about 9 million (about 5 percent) in 2033, CBO and JCT estimate. Employment would increase as the labor force expanded, because the additional population would add to demand for goods and services and, in turn, to the demand for labor. However, temporary imbalances in the skills and occupations demanded and supplied in the labor market, as well as other factors, would cause the unemployment rate to be slightly higher for several years than projected under current law.

The increase in average wages for the entire labor force in 2025 and later years relative to average wages under current law would occur primarily because the bill would boost the productivity of labor and capital (as discussed below). However, not all

---

7. Throughout this report, the term "immigration" is used to refer to people who come to the country on either a permanent basis or a temporary basis. In addition, the phrase "new immigrants" refers to net new immigrants under S. 744—that is, the additional people who would immigrate under the legislation less the people who would immigrate under current law but not under the legislation. For further discussion of the terminology of immigration law and the net flows of people under S. 744, see CBO's cost estimate for the legislation.

workers would experience those effects equally. The legislation would particularly increase the number of workers with lower or higher skills but would have less effect on the number of workers with average skills. As a result, the wages of lower- and higher-skilled workers would tend to be pushed downward slightly (by less than ½ percent) relative to the wages of workers with average skills.

The increase in the average wage would not occur for a dozen years. As the labor supply initially increased under the legislation, less capital would be available for each worker to produce output, and thus workers' output, on average, would be lower for a time. That decline would reduce average wages relative to those under current law. Over time, as capital investment increased and the amount of capital per worker returned approximately to what it would have been under current law—and productivity improved as well—average wages would be higher than under current law.

Investment and Interest Rates. Capital investment would rise primarily because the return that investors would earn on a given amount of investment would be higher under the legislation than under current law, for two reasons: First, the larger labor force would render the existing stock of capital relatively scarce (compared with the supply of labor). Second, even apart from capital's relative scarcity, each unit of capital, such as a single computer, would be more productive (as discussed below). Relative to that projected under current law, the nation's capital stock would be about 2 percent greater in 2023 and about 5 percent greater in 2033, according to CBO's central estimates.

The increase in the rate of return on investment would moderate over time as the stock of capital grew. For roughly the first decade, the increase in the size of the labor force would make capital relatively scarce. By the second decade, changes to the labor force would become proportionately smaller and the capital stock would grow sufficiently for its rate of return to move down toward, although not quite reaching, the rate that would prevail under current law. With that greater rate of earnings on investment, the federal government would face higher interest rates than under current law because it would be competing with the private sector for investors' money.

Productivity. In CBO's view, enactment of S. 744 would lead to slightly higher productivity of both labor and capital because the increase in immigration—particularly of highly skilled immigrants—would tend to generate additional technological advancements, such as new inventions and improvements in production processes. CBO estimates that total factor productivity (TFP, the average real output per unit of combined labor and capital services) would be higher by roughly 0.7 percent in 2023 and by roughly 1.0 percent in 2033, compared with what would occur under current law. The increase in TFP would make workers and capital alike more productive, leading to higher GDP, higher wages, and higher interest rates.

Effects on Employment and Wages

Enacting S. 744 would cause changes in at least four aspects of the labor market:

- The size of the labor force,

- Average wages,

- Relative wages for workers with different skills, and

- Employment and unemployment.

The Size of the Labor Force

If S. 744 was enacted, CBO estimates, the U.S. population would be larger by about 10 million people in 2023 and by about 16 million people in 2033 than projected under current law. Slightly more than two-thirds of those additional residents would be adults.

CBO and JCT expect that the new adults would participate in the labor force at a higher rate, on average, than do adults in the current population. Many additional adults entering the country under the bill would, as required in the legislation, enter the country with employment. Most other adults who entered would participate in the labor force at a rate similar to that of the existing foreign-born population, CBO and JCT project.[8] However, some of the additional adult entrants under S. 744 would tend to have lower labor force participation—such as those age 65 or older, and, from among the people whose visa applications are part of the existing backlog, those who would join family members already working in this country.

Altogether, CBO and JCT estimate that, under S. 744, the labor force would be about 6 million (roughly 3½ percent) larger in 2023 and about 9 million (roughly 5 percent) larger in 2033 than it would be under current law.

Average Wages

If S. 744 was enacted, average wages would be lower by about 0.1 percent in 2023 and higher by about 0.5 percent in 2033 than projected under current law, according to CBO's central estimates. Wages would be lower than under current law through 2024. That small initial reduction in average wages would occur primarily because the amount of capital available to workers would not increase as rapidly as the number of workers and because the new workers would be less skilled and have lower wages, on average, than the workers under current law. In later years, however, the expanding

---

8. Among current immigrants in the United States, men age 16 or older are more likely than are native-born men to be working or looking for work (that is, to be in the labor force), whereas women in the same age group are less likely than native-born women to be in the labor force. Specifically, in 2012, 79 percent of foreign-born men age 16 or older were in the labor force, compared with 69 percent of native-born men, and 55 percent of foreign-born women age 16 or older were in the labor force, compared with 58 percent of native-born women. For additional information on the labor force participation of the current immigrant population, see Congressional Budget Office, letter to the Honorable Paul Ryan concerning a description of the immigrant population—2013 update (May 8, 2013), www.cbo.gov/publication/44134.

capital stock would return the ratio of capital to labor to near its level under current law (as discussed later in this report). Moreover, total factor productivity would be higher.

S. 744 would allow significantly more workers with low skills and with high skills to enter the United States—through, for example, new programs for temporary workers and an increase in the number of workers eligible for H-1B visas—and would allow somewhat greater numbers of workers with skills in the middle of the distribution to enter as well.[9] Taking into account all of those flows of new immigrants, CBO and JCT expect that a greater number of immigrants with lower skills than with higher skills would be added to the workforce, slightly pushing down the average wage for the labor force as a whole, other things being equal.[10]

However, CBO and JCT expect that currently unauthorized workers who would obtain legal status under S. 744 would see an increase in their average wages. The bill's effect on revenues as reported in the cost estimate incorporates an increase in average wages of 12 percent for unauthorized workers who attain legal residency. Their wages would rise both because such workers would have a stronger bargaining position with their employers and because they would be able to find jobs that better fit their skills and education and thus become more productive.[11] (The portion of the increase in average wages attributable to higher labor productivity is reflected in an increase in GDP; that attributable to an improved bargaining position is reflected in a decrease in profits.)

Because the bill would increase the rate of growth of the labor force, average wages would be held down in the first decade after enactment by a reduction in the ratio of capital to labor, which would make workers less productive—and therefore lower their

---

9. For more information on the changes in immigration rules under S. 744, see CBO's cost estimate for the legislation.

10. Differences in earnings among immigrants and native-born workers tend to diminish over time as immigrants acquire skills, such as fluency in the English language, that are important to success in the U.S. labor market. CBO did not incorporate such changes in wages over time into its analysis. See George J. Borjas, *The Slowdown in the Economic Assimilation of Immigrants: Aging and Cohort Effects Revisited Again*, Working Paper 19116 (National Bureau of Economic Research, June 2013), www.nber.org/papers/w19116.

11. According to a study of the effects on the wages of workers who gained legal status as a result of the 1986 Immigration Reform and Control Act, "the postlegalization changes in wage determinants for legalized workers are consistent with labor market mobility, which provides workers with an opportunity to move into jobs that reward existing human capital." See Sherrie A. Kossoudji and Deborah A. Cobb-Clark, "Coming Out of the Shadows: Learning About Legal Status and Wages From the Legalized Population," *Journal of Labor Economics*, vol. 20, no. 3 (July 2002), p. 618, http://tinyurl.com/kaqesty.

wages, on average, relative to what would occur under current law.[12] Although investment and thus the capital stock would begin to increase quickly, the capital-to-labor ratio would be lower for roughly the first decade. The rate of additional investment—and thus the speed at which the capital stock grew—would help determine how quickly average wages would rebound to the level that would prevail under current law.

CBO's and JCT's cost estimate for S. 744 includes the budgetary effects of changes in average wages from the gradual response of the size of the capital stock to the increase in the labor force (but not from the increase in total factor productivity or the additional growth in the capital stock resulting from the increase in TFP, which is discussed below).

Relative Wages

In addition to its impact on average overall wages in the economy, S. 744 would have varying effects on relative wages of people at different levels of skill.[13] If S. 744 was enacted, CBO expects, the larger increase in the number of workers with lower or higher skills relative to the number of people with average skills would slightly reduce the relative wages of workers with lower and higher skills; that is, the average wage paid to workers with lower or higher skills would fall relative to the average wage of the labor force as a whole. Specifically, CBO estimates that, by 2033, S. 744 would lead to a decline of 0.3 percent in the relative wages for workers in the lowest quintile (the bottom fifth) of the skill distribution—typically, workers who did not finish high school and some portion of high school graduates—and for workers in the highest quintile—typically, college graduates and workers with postgraduate degrees. In contrast, CBO estimates that average wages for workers in the middle three quintiles (typically, a portion of high school and college graduates and workers with some postsecondary education) would increase by 0.5 percent relative to overall average wages.

It bears emphasizing that those figures are estimated effects on the *distribution* of wages and not on the overall level of wages. As discussed above, CBO estimates that average wages would be affected by other factors, including changes in the capital-to-labor ratio and total factor productivity, which would have roughly the same impact

---

12. The current analysis discusses two kinds of productivity: *Labor productivity*, which measures the amount of goods and services that can be produced per hour of labor (and reflects the skill of workers, the amount of capital each worker uses, and total factor productivity) and *total factor productivity*, which reflects the efficiency with which labor and capital combine to produce goods and services (and can increase because of inventions, new processes, and new organizational structures, for example). CBO estimates that S. 744 would affect both kinds of productivity.

13. The relative wage of workers in a skill group is the ratio of the average wage for that skill group divided by the average wage in the economy as a whole. An increase in the relative wage of a group means the group's average wage rose more (or fell less) than the average wage of all workers; a decline in a group's relative wage means the opposite. For example, if the overall average wage rises by 1.0 percent but the average wage of less-skilled workers rises by only 0.7 percent, the relative wage of the less-skilled would have fallen by 0.3 percent.

on wages for people of various skill levels. By 2033, when CBO estimates that average wages in the labor force would be about 0.5 percent higher under S. 744 than under current law, average wages would be higher under the bill than under current law for workers in all quintiles of the skill distribution, even after allowing for the estimated distributional effects.

The estimates of the bill's effects on relative wages are based on CBO's estimates of the changes in the supply of workers with different amounts of skill and on a review of empirical research on the historical relationship between immigration and the wage distribution. An appendix to this report briefly summarizes that review and its application to this analysis of S. 744.

Employment and Unemployment

CBO estimates that S. 744 would cause the unemployment rate to increase slightly between 2014 and 2020, relative to the rate projected under current law, but to have no effect on the unemployment rate after 2020. The slight increase over the next several years, the impact of which is incorporated into the cost estimate, would arise from three different sources:

- CBO expects that the arrival of new immigrants would cause a short-term imbalance between the types of workers needed to produce the goods and services demanded in the economy and the skills and occupations of available workers. Some movement of workers to new jobs would be required to restore equilibrium, but such a process causes short-term unemployment as workers search for new jobs that best match their skills and interests.

- Although the average wage would be lower than under current law over the first dozen years, the minimum wage would keep the wages of some less-skilled workers from falling, dampening businesses' demand for those workers.[14]

- While the economy adjusted to the increased inflow of immigrants, the increase in demand for labor could lag behind the increase in demand for goods and services.

Those effects would prevent employment from rising by the full increase in the labor force during a period of transition. As a result, enacting S. 744 would raise the unemployment rate over the next five years by up to roughly 0.1 percentage point

---

14. Under both current law and S. 744, the minimum wage would affect fewer workers over time as rising productivity and inflation tend to push up the wages of lower-skilled workers relative to the minimum wage.

relative to projections under current law; the rate would remain slightly elevated through 2020, CBO estimates.[15]

The unemployment rate also might be affected during the next few years if the legislation boosted overall demand for goods and services by more or less than their potential supply, but CBO expects the effects on demand and potential supply to roughly balance. Spending by new immigrants, in part financed by the resources those immigrants would bring with them, would increase demand for goods and services in the United States. Because only some of those new immigrants would participate in the labor force, the proportionate increase in demand could be larger than the increase in labor supply. By contrast, if a substantial share of the earnings of new immigrants was sent abroad as remittances or if new immigrants had high saving rates, the additional supply of labor by immigrants could be proportionally larger than the boost in the need for labor stemming from greater demand for goods and services. CBO expects those factors to be roughly offsetting.

The current slack in the economy would not notably influence the economic effects of S. 744, including its effects on employment and unemployment, in part because only a small part of the bill's total effect on immigration is expected to occur over the next two years, when the slack is projected to be especially large. That slack does imply, however, that over the next few years, new immigrants would have a higher unemployment rate than their natural rate—the rate of unemployment arising from all sources except fluctuations in aggregate demand—just as is true for the existing population under CBO's current-law projections.[16]

In the long run, the actual unemployment rate in the economy tends to be close to its natural rate. The natural rate of unemployment of the additional immigrants would be comparable, on average, to that of the current population, CBO expects, so there would be little effect on the unemployment rate in the long run. Thus, in the long run, the number of employed people would increase by the same percentage as the

---

15. For research on the effects of immigration on employment and unemployment, see Giovanni Peri, "The Effect of Immigration on Productivity: Evidence from U.S. States," *Review of Economics and Statistics*, vol. 94, no. 1 (February 2012), pp. 348–358, http://tinyurl.com/pbqfava; Madeline Zavodny, *Immigration and American Jobs* (American Enterprise Institute for Public Policy Research and Partnership for a New American Economy, 2011), www.renewoureconomy.org/aeireport; George J. Borjas, Jeffrey Grogger, and Gordon H. Hanson, "Immigration and the Economic Status of African-American Men," *Economica*, vol. 77, no. 306 (April 2010), pp. 255–282, http://tinyurl.com/q2t7sem; David Card, "Is the New Immigration Really So Bad?" *Economic Journal*, vol. 115, no. 507 (November 2005), pp. F300–F323, http://tinyurl.com/pcva26a; and David Card "Immigrant Inflows, Native Outflows, and the Local Labor Market Impacts of Higher Immigration," *Journal of Labor Economics*, vol. 19, no. 1 (January 2001), pp. 22–64, http://tinyurl.com/o3y5zwd.

16. When projecting the bill's effect on immigration, CBO considered the strength of the economy, particularly in light of the recent slowdown in immigration that is attributable to the weakness in the economy.

growth in the labor force—by about 3½ percent in 2023 and by about 5 percent in 2033, CBO estimates.

Particular provisions of S. 744 would affect employment in various sectors of the economy differently. For example, provisions that would allow an increase in the number of highly skilled workers would boost the number of such workers who were employed by a greater percentage than the overall increase in employment. In addition, the increase in wages projected beginning in 2025 would encourage greater labor force participation and hours of work, relative to what would prevail under current law.

Effects on Capital Investment and Interest Rates

If S. 744 was enacted, the capital stock would be larger than under current law—by about 2 percent in 2023 and by about 5 percent in 2033, according to CBO's central estimates. The increase in investment that would generate that larger capital stock would be primarily financed by greater private saving than would occur under current law. CBO's analysis also takes account of changes in public saving; private and public saving together represent the main influences on the sources of funds for domestic investment in productive resources such as equipment and structures.[17]

Enacting S. 744 would lead to an increase in private saving for two reasons in particular. First, output and incomes would increase, primarily because of the larger workforce and the boost to total factor productivity, but also because of the increased earnings of currently unauthorized workers who attain legal status. Workers would save some of their additional income, thus increasing the amount of money available for investment. Second, the rate of return on capital would rise because the increase in the supply of labor relative to the stock of capital, along with the increase in TFP, would boost the productivity of capital. The higher rate of return would encourage people to save a larger share of their income, further increasing the amount of money available for investment.

The legislation also would affect public saving through its impact on the federal budget deficit. Higher deficits subtract from the funds available for private-sector investment because more of those funds are used instead to purchase government bonds; smaller deficits have the opposite effect. CBO's economic analysis incorporates the decrease in the deficit from the effects of S. 744 on direct spending and revenue (as reported in the cost estimate); it also incorporates the decrease in the deficit from the incremental budgetary effects of changes in the economy that the cost estimate does not reflect.

Public saving also could change because the influx of new immigrants would cause state and local governments to experience both greater demand for services and an increase in revenues, potentially affecting their budget balances. However, CBO has

---

17. Private saving is saving by households and businesses; public saving is the net amount of surpluses or deficits of state and local governments and the federal government.

not analyzed the full effects of S. 744 on the budgets of state and local governments, and in any case, the direct effects of the legislation might be offset by other policy changes that would result from requirements in many states to maintain balanced budgets. Therefore, CBO's analysis in this report does not incorporate any change in the projected budget balances of state or local governments.

The capital stock would increase slowly over time, relative to current law, if S. 744 was enacted because new investments would be small relative to the total stock of capital in the U.S. economy. That slow adjustment of the capital stock relative to the labor force would keep capital relatively scarce. That effect, along with an increase in TFP that would boost the productivity of capital, would lead to an increase in the rate of return on investment in capital. According to CBO's estimates, those rates of return would remain above current-law projections throughout the next two decades. With that higher return on investment, the federal government would face higher interest rates than under current law because it would be competing with the private sector for investors' money.

Effects on Productivity

Total factor productivity measures the efficiency with which labor and capital combine to produce goods and services, and its growth over time can be thought of as a measure of the rate of technological advancement. TFP rises, for example, with invention and with improvements in production processes. CBO projects that the additional immigration resulting from S. 744 would raise TFP by roughly 0.7 percent in 2023 and by roughly 1.0 percent in 2033, relative to the agency's projections under current law. Although the determinants of TFP are poorly understood, empirical research broadly suggests that an influx of immigrants, particularly highly skilled immigrants, would lead to increased innovation and task specialization. And those improvements in turn would increase economic output for any given supply of labor and capital stock.

A substantial body of research documents certain effects of highly skilled immigrants on the U.S. economy. For example, although immigrants constituted just 12 percent of the population in 2000, they accounted for 26 percent of U.S.-based Nobel Prize winners between 1990 and 2000, and they made up 25 percent of the founders of public-venture–backed companies started between 1990 and 2005. Moreover, immigrants receive patents at twice the rate of the native-born U.S. population.[18] Logic suggests that such accomplishments should boost TFP, but quantifications of that connection are few. In one example, however, researchers demonstrated a strong correlation between the research and development undertaken by scientists and engineers and the rate of growth in TFP, implying a boost to TFP from an increase in the number of people working in fields that are related to technological innovation, such as science, technology, engineering, or mathematics.[19]

CBO's estimate of the effect of S. 744 on TFP reflects the estimates reported in a small body of research that quantifies the effects of increases in immigration on the economic output of existing labor and capital. Those estimates fall broadly into three areas. One area is exemplified by a finding that a rise in the immigration of college-educated workers leads to a greater number of patents issued—including to workers in the native-born population—suggesting positive spillover effects on the existing population's ability to innovate.[20] Another area of study is exemplified by a report indicating that an increase in the number of immigrant workers, regardless of skill, leads to higher total factor productivity because of an increase in task specialization and other improvements.[21] A third area of study examines occupation-specific immigration, attempting to identify evidence that an increase in immigration creates a positive spillover for workers in a specific occupation. Several studies examining that question have found no effect of immigration on TFP.[22] In undertaking the analysis of S. 744, CBO combined the results of those three areas of study, drawing more heavily on the literature demonstrating a connection between greater immigration of certain skilled workers and increased TFP.

The increase in TFP that CBO projects would accrue if S. 744 was enacted would lead to increases in GDP, average wages, and capital income. However, CBO projects that TFP would rise slowly relative to current law as the effects of the bill on the labor force occurred gradually.

---

18. See Jennifer Hunt and Marjolaine Gauthier-Loiselle, "How Much Does Immigration Boost Innovation?" *American Economic Journal: Macroeconomics*, vol. 2, no. 2 (April 2010), pp. 31–56, http://tinyurl.com/lclzghn; Stuart Anderson and Michaela Platzer, *American Made: The Impact of Immigrant Entrepreneurs and Professionals on U.S. Competitiveness* (National Venture Capital Association, 2006), http://tinyurl.com/k7h7d8o; and Paula E. Stephan and Sharon G. Levin, "Exceptional Contributions to U.S. Science by the Foreign-Born and Foreign-Educated," *Population Research and Policy Review*, vol. 20, no. 1–2 (April 2001): pp. 59–79, http://tinyurl.com/luz5k2w. Related additional research includes that by Jennifer Hunt, "Which Immigrants Are Most Innovative and Entrepreneurial? Distinctions by Entry Visa," *Journal of Labor Economics*, vol. 29, no. 3 (July 2011), pp. 417–457, http://tinyurl.com/m3dpjpl; and George J. Borjas, "The Labor-Market Impact of High-Skill Immigration," *American Economic Review*, vol. 95, no. 2 (May 2005): pp. 56–60, http://tinyurl.com/n2zz6k9.

19. Charles I. Jones, "Sources of U.S. Economic Growth in a World of Ideas," *American Economic Review*, vol. 92, no. 1 (March 2002), http://tinyurl.com/k24ne3u.

20. Jennifer Hunt and Marjolaine Gauthier-Loiselle, "How Much Does Immigration Boost Innovation?" *American Economic Journal: Macroeconomics*, vol. 2, no. 2 (April 2010), pp. 31–56, http://tinyurl.com/lclzghn.

21. Giovanni Peri, "The Effect of Immigration on Productivity: Evidence from U.S. States," *Review of Economics and Statistics*, vol. 94, no. 1 (February 23012), pp. 348–358 http://tinyurl.com/pbqfava.

22. George J. Borjas and Kirk B. Doran, "The Collapse of the Soviet Union and the Productivity of American Mathematicians," *Quarterly Journal of Economics*, vol. 127, no. 3 (August 2012), pp. 1143–1203, http://tinyurl.com/kybqfsr; Fabian Waldinger, "Peer Effects in Science: Evidence From the Dismissal of Scientists in Nazi Germany," *Review of Economic Studies*, vol. 79, no. 2 (April 2012), pp. 838–861, http://tinyurl.com/mjjaqgg; and William R. Kerr and William F. Lincoln, "The Supply Side of Innovation: H-1B Visa Reforms and U.S. Ethnic Invention," *Journal of Labor Economics*, vol. 28, no. 3 (July 2010), pp. 473–508, http://tinyurl.com/kl4bt65.

Ranges of Estimated Economic Effects

To estimate the overall economic effects of S. 744, CBO employed an enhanced version of a widely used model developed by Robert Solow. In that model, output depends on the quantity and quality of the labor force, the size and composition of the capital stock, and the nation's technological progress. CBO produced a range of estimates by applying alternative assumptions about the degree to which economic variables influence households' decisions about how much to work and save—specifically, about how people would adjust the number of hours they worked in response to changes in average wage rates and how each dollar of change in the federal deficit as a result of S. 744 would affect domestic investment.[23] The ranges of estimates are intended to cover, on a judgmental basis, about two-thirds of the possible outcomes for those economic relationships. Still, the effects of S. 744 on the economy and the federal budget would be complicated and highly uncertain, even in the short run, and as a result the actual effects could be well outside CBO's ranges of estimates. In particular, two major sources of uncertainty not reflected in the range of estimates would be the bill's effects on the labor force and productivity over the next two decades.

Real GDP would be greater by 3.3 percent in 2023 and by 5.4 percent in 2033 if the bill was enacted, according to CBO's central estimates of the overall economic impact of the legislation (see Figure 1 on page 17). Under the full range of the two key economic relationships in CBO's analysis, CBO estimates that the bill could boost GDP by an amount between 5.1 percent to 5.7 percent in 2033.

The effects of the legislation on real GNP would be slightly smaller because increases in the rate of return on capital and in interest rates would imply greater flows of profits and interest to foreigners. According to CBO's central estimates, real GNP would be greater by 2.4 percent in 2023 and by 4.5 percent in 2033. Under the full range of estimates, the bill could boost GNP by an amount between 4.1 percent and 4.8 percent in 2033.

Because the population would expand considerably, per capita GNP would rise by much less than would total GNP. According to CBO's central estimates, S. 744 would reduce per capita GNP by 0.7 percent in 2023 and raise it by 0.2 percent in 2033 (see Figure 2 on page 18). Under the full range of estimates, the bill could lower per capita GNP in 2033 by as much as 0.2 percent or raise it by as much as 0.6 percent.

---

23. For a more detailed discussion of CBO's approach to modeling the long-term economic effects of changes in federal policies, see Congressional Budget Office, *The Economic Impact of the President's 2013 Budget* (April 2012), Appendix, www.cbo.gov/publication/42972; and *How the Supply of Labor Responds to Fiscal Policy* (October 2012), www.cbo.gov/publication/43674. For labor supply, the earnings-weighted substitution elasticity ranges from 0.16 to 0.32, and the income elasticity ranges from -0.10 to zero. Each additional dollar of deficit leads to a decline in domestic investment that ranges from $0.15 to $0.50. The range of macroeconomic effects was calculated as the minimum and maximum of four estimates—corresponding to low and high labor supply elasticities and to low and high effects of deficits on investment, respectively.

Because of both the slow adjustment of the capital stock to the additional growth of the labor force and the increase in TFP, CBO expects that the return on investment would remain above current-law projections throughout the next two decades. With that higher return on investment, the federal government would face higher interest rates than under current law. According to the agency's central estimates, enacting the bill would increase interest rates by 0.4 percentage points in 2023 and by 0.3 percentage points in 2033. Under the full range of estimates, interest rates would increase by 0.3 percentage points to 0.4 percentage points in 2033.

Average wages would be lower by 0.1 percent in 2023 and higher by 0.5 percent in 2033 compared with average wages under current law, according to CBO's central estimates. Under the full range of estimates, average wages would increase by 0.3 percent to 0.8 percent in 2033.

Federal Budgetary Consequences of the Economic Effects Not Included in the Cost Estimate

S. 744 would directly affect the federal budget and significantly affect the economy as well; those economic changes would in turn affect the federal budget. CBO and JCT's cost estimate reflects all of the direct federal budgetary effects and some, but not all, of the feedback effects on the budget that would result from the bill's impact on the economy. In particular, CBO's and JCT's cost estimate includes the increase in federal revenues that would stem directly from taxing the earnings of new immigrants and from taxing the additional taxable earnings that would arise from the change in status of currently unauthorized residents. It does not, however, include any budgetary effects attributable to changes in the productivity of labor and capital, the income earned by capital, the rate of return on capital (and therefore on the interest rate on government debt), or the differences in wages for workers with different skills.

CBO estimated those additional budgetary impacts using a simplified analysis that accounts for changes in taxable income and in interest rates, among other things, but that does not incorporate the sort of detailed program-by-program analysis that the agency uses for official cost estimates. The additional budgetary impacts in CBO's estimates arise from two factors:

■ Changes in output that would affect revenues by altering the amount of workers' taxable income (CBO and JCT's cost estimate includes some but not all of that effect because it incorporates only a portion of the total estimated effect on output); and

■ Changes in interest rates that would raise the federal government's borrowing costs.[24]

---

24. Cost estimates for legislation show the changes in the costs of programs and revenues that would result from enacting the legislation but not the interest costs or savings for any changes in borrowing by the government. To be consistent with that approach, the estimated effects on federal interest payments in this analysis reflect only the impact of *changes in interest rates* and exclude the effects of *changes in the amount of debt* that would be attributable to the enactment of S. 744.

CBO's estimates of the additional budgetary impacts of S. 744 also account for other effects, such as how changes in the mix of labor income and capital income would affect revenues and how the estimated changes in workers' relative wages would lead to slightly higher government transfer payments to low-income households (in the form of food assistance and medical benefits, for example) and slightly lower income tax revenues.[25]

According to CBO's central estimates, the economic effects of the legislation that are not incorporated in the cost estimate would increase federal budget deficits by about $30 billion over the 2014–2018 period and decrease deficits by about $30 billion from 2019 through 2023, leaving the deficit roughly unchanged for the 2014–2023 period. For the next decade, 2024 through 2033, the economic effects of the legislation that are not incorporated in the cost estimate would reduce federal budget deficits by about $300 billion. (By way of comparison, CBO estimates that, under current law, total GDP during the 2024–2033 period would be roughly $330 trillion.)

---

25. The estimated budgetary impact of changes in relative wages would increase deficits by less than $5 billion over the 2014–2023 period and by roughly $10 billion over the 2024–2033 period.

Figure 1.

Estimated Effects of S. 744 on Real GDP

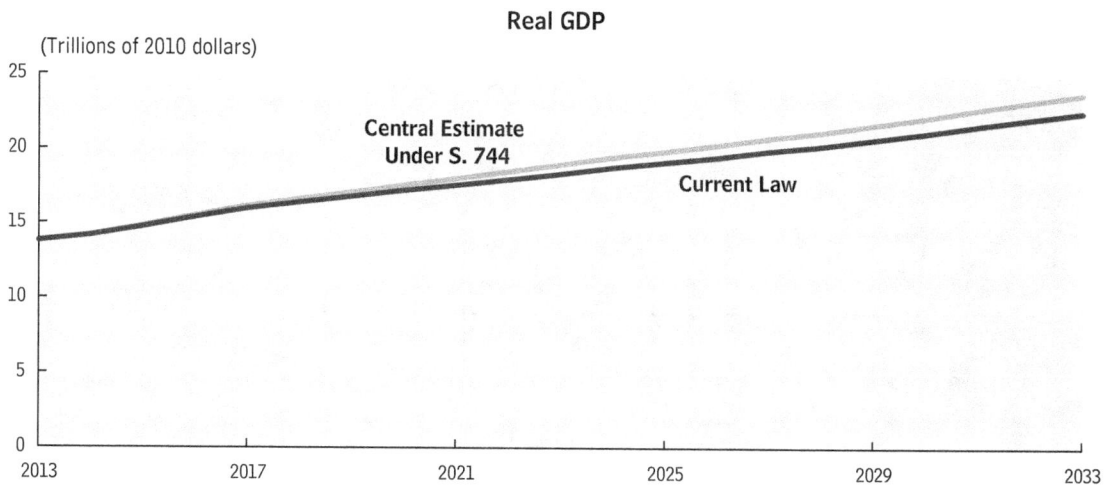

Real GDP

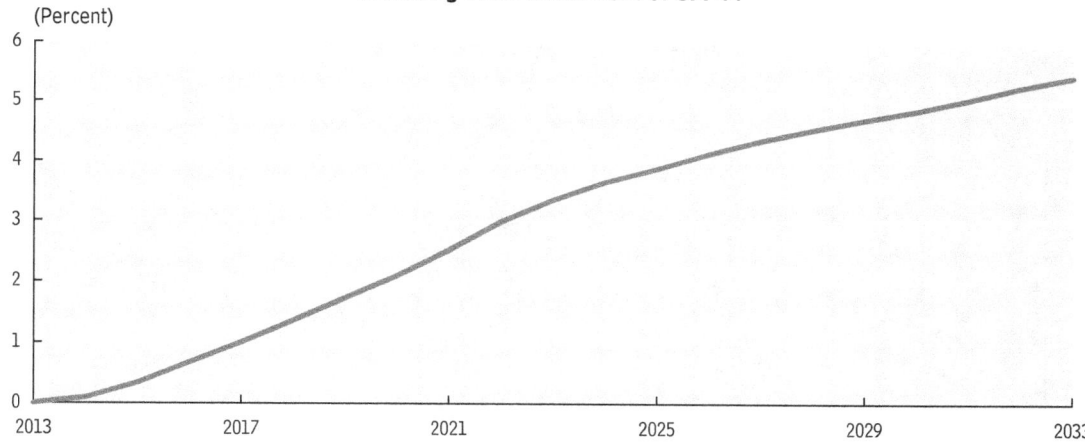

**Central Estimate of the Increase in Real GDP
Resulting From Enactment of S. 744**

Source: Congressional Budget Office.

Notes: The central estimate incorporates CBO's central assumptions about the effect of deficits on investment and the effect of wage rates on the labor supply.

Current-law projections are made under the assumption that current laws and policies generally remain in place.

Projections are annual and are plotted through 2033.

S. 744 = the Border Security, Economic Opportunity, and Immigration Modernization Act; real GDP = inflation-adjusted gross domestic product.

Figure 2.

Estimated Effects of S. 744 on Per Capita Real GNP and on Average Wages

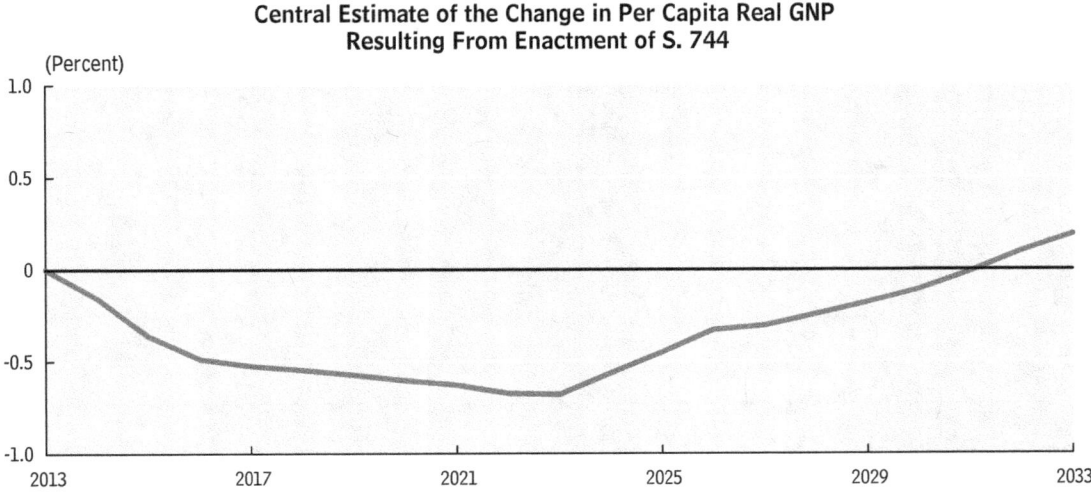

Central Estimate of the Change in Per Capita Real GNP Resulting From Enactment of S. 744

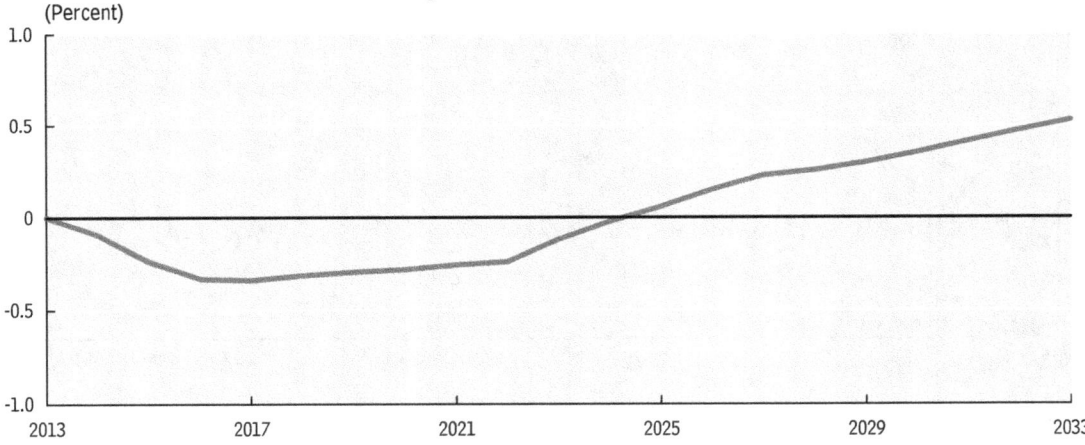

Central Estimate of the Change in Average Wages Resulting From Enactment of S. 744

Source: Congressional Budget Office.

Notes: Central estimates incorporate CBO's central assumptions about the effect of deficits on investment and the effect of wage rates on the labor supply.

Current-law projections are made under the assumption that current laws and policies generally remain in place.

Projections are annual and are plotted through 2033.

GNP is a measure of output that differs from gross domestic product primarily by including the capital income that residents earn from investments abroad and excluding the capital income that nonresidents earn from domestic investment. Changes in GNP are therefore a better measure of the effects of policies on U.S. residents' income than are changes in gross domestic product.

S. 744 = the Border Security, Economic Opportunity, and Immigration Modernization Act; GNP = gross national product.

Appendix:
Effects of the Legislation on
Relative Wages

Research concerning the effects of immigration on relative wages generally examines how wages are affected by the possibility of substituting workers with different skills. If two types of workers are perfect substitutes, then increasing the supply of one type of worker reduces the relative wages of the other, holding everything else in the economy unchanged; if two types of workers are instead complements, then increasing the supply of one type will increase the relative wages of the other. Those effects can differ by the amount of skill workers have, and they can depend on the distribution of skills among new immigrant workers and those in the existing labor force.

One body of research asserts that although workers with and without high school diplomas are imperfect substitutes, native and immigrant workers are perfect substitutes. One example of that research finds that, over the period from 1980 to 2000, an increase of 1 percent in the labor supply attributable to immigration was correlated with a 0.5 percent decline in relative wages for workers without a high school education, a 0.2 percent decline in wages for college graduates, and an increase of 0.1 percent to 0.3 percent in the relative wages of high school graduates and workers with some college education.[1]

Another body of research indicates that workers with and without a high school diploma are perfect substitutes and that native-born and immigrant workers are imperfect substitutes. One example of that research reports that between 1990 and 2006, a 1 percent increase in the labor supply attributable to immigration was correlated with an increase in relative wages of about 0.1 percent for native-born workers without a high school diploma, with virtually no change in relative wages for college graduates, and with a slight increase in relative wages for native-born workers with a high school diploma or some college education.[2] That research also shows that the relative wages of past immigrants declined the most in response to increases in

---

1. George J. Borjas, "The Labor Demand Curve Is Downward Sloping: Reexamining the Impact of Immigration on the Labor Market," *Quarterly Journal of Economics*, vol. 118, no. 4 (November 2003), pp. 1335–1374, http://tinyurl.com/mqgxox8. For a discussion of relative wage effects of similar magnitude for the 1900–2000 period for immigrants from Mexico, see George J. Borjas and Lawrence F. Katz, "The Evolution of the Mexican-Born Workforce in the United States," in George J. Borjas, ed., *Mexican Immigration to the United States* (National Bureau of Economic Research, 2007), pp. 13–56, http://papers.nber.org/books/borj06-1.

2. Gianmarco I.P. Ottaviano and Giovanni Peri, "Rethinking the Effect of Immigration on Wages," *Journal of the European Economic Association*, vol. 10, no. 1 (January 2012), pp. 152–197, http://tinyurl.com/nvthkw8.

immigration because the groups of past and new immigrants are more easily substituted for one another than are other groups of workers.[3]

Historically, immigration has been greatest among the least and most skilled workers. As a result, a broad range of research suggests that the relative wages of workers with higher and lower skills tend to fall in response to immigration. Based on CBO's reading of that research, a 1 percent increase in the labor force attributable to immigration has tended to lower the relative wages for all workers with less than a high school diploma by roughly 0.3 percent, to leave the relative wages for high school graduates roughly unchanged, to raise the relative wages for workers with some college education by roughly 0.1 percent, and to lower the relative wages for workers with at least a college degree by roughly 0.1 percent.[4]

CBO estimated the effect of S. 744 on relative wages by applying those estimates to the estimated effects of the bill on the labor force. The legislation would particularly increase the supply of workers in the top and the bottom quintiles of the skill distribution: The top quintile would be expected to include highly trained immigrants, such as those who would be eligible for H-1B visas, and the bottom quintile would be expected to include largely untrained workers, including those who would seek temporary employment. Immigrants in the middle three quintiles of the skill distribution would make up a relatively small share of those joining the U.S. labor force as a result of S. 744. Based on the findings in the literature, CBO estimates that relative wages would decrease modestly for workers in the top and bottom quintiles of the skill distribution and that they would rise modestly for the middle quintiles.

---

3.   For another example of research that shows a larger effect on the relative wages of prior immigrants, see Heidi Shierholz, *Immigration and Wages: Methodological Advancements Confirm Modest Gains for Native Workers*, Briefing Paper 255 (Economic Policy Institute, February 2010), www.epi.org/publication/bp255/.

4.   In addition to the publications already mentioned, see Christian Dustmann, Tommaso Frattini, and Ian P. Preston, "The Effect of Immigration Along the Distribution of Wages," *Review of Economic Studies*, vol. 80, no. 1 (January 2013), pp. 145–173, http://tinyurl.com/lv8ms2g; George Borjas and others, "Comment: On Estimating Elasticities of Substitution," *Journal of the European Economic Association*, vol. 10, no. 1 (January 2012), pp. 198–210, http://tinyurl.com/oc53sl3; and Giovanni Peri and Chad Sparber, "Task Specialization, Immigration, and Wages," *American Economic Journal: Applied Economics*, vol. 1, no. 3 (July 2009), pp. 135–169, http://tinyurl.com/lre8c95.

About This Document

This report provides information to supplement CBO and JCT's cost estimate for S. 744, the Border Security, Economic Opportunity, and Immigration Modernization Act. In keeping with CBO's mandate to provide objective, impartial analysis, the report makes no recommendations.

Benjamin Page and Felix Reichling wrote the report, with guidance from Wendy Edelberg and Kim Kowalewski. The underlying economic and budgetary analysis was conducted by dozens of analysts at CBO and by the staff of the Joint Committee on Taxation. George Borjas of Harvard University, Gordon Hansen of the University of California at San Diego, Lawrence Katz of Harvard University, and Giovanni Peri of the University of California at Davis provided feedback on the analysis. Their assistance implies no responsibility for the final product, which rests solely with CBO.

Kate Kelly edited the report, and Maureen Costantino and Jeanine Rees prepared it for publication. An electronic version is available on CBO's website (www.cbo.gov).

Douglas W. Elmendorf
Director

June 2013

www.ingramcontent.com/pod-product-compliance
Lightning Source LLC
Chambersburg PA
CBHW080404290526
45790CB00009BA/3694